The 1900s
Britain in Pictures

The 1900s
Britain in Pictures

PA Photos

AMMONITE
PRESS

First Published 2008 by
Ammonite Press
an imprint of AE Publications Ltd,
166 High Street, Lewes, East Sussex BN7 1XU

Text copyright Ammonite Press
Images copyright PA Photos
Copyright in the work Ammonite Press

ISBN 978-1-906672-06-5

British Cataloguing in Publication Data. A catalogue
record of this book is available from the British Library.

Editor: Paul Richardson
Picture research: PA Photos
Design: Gravemaker + Scott

Colour reproduction by GMC Reprographics
Printed by Colorprint, China

Page 2: Suffragettes
marching to protest the
first arrest of a suffragette in
London.
1908

Page 5: Colonel Samuel
Cody in British Army
Aeroplane No. 1 during the
first British powered flight.
The flight lasted 27 seconds
and covered a distance of
1,390ft over Farnborough
Common.
16th October, 1908

Page 6: London Olympics:
Italy's Pietri Dorando
staggers across the line
to win the marathon. The
officials who helped him for
the last few hundred yards –
leading to his disqualification
– can be seen to his left
and right.
24th July, 1908

Introduction

The archives of PA Photos yield a unique insight into Britain's recent past. Thanks to the science of photography we can view the 20th Century more accurately than any that came before, but it is thanks to news photography, and in particular the great news agency that is The Press Association, that we are able now to witness the events that made up life in Britain, not so long ago.

It is easy, looking back, to imagine a past neatly partitioned into clearly defined periods and dominated by landmarks: wars, political upheaval and economic trends. But the archive tells a different story: alongside the major events that constitute formal history are found the smaller things that had equal – if not greater – significance for ordinary people at the time. And while the photographers were working for that moment's news rather than posterity, the camera is an undiscriminating eye that records everything in its view: to modern eyes it is often the backgrounds of these pictures, not their intended subjects, that provide the greatest fascination.

The country began the new century with tremendous confidence: it was felt there was nothing this great nation couldn't do, and that the rest of the world naturally accepted Britain's supremacy. Perhaps the most significant indication of how misplaced was this confidence came with the disastrous 1908 London Olympic Games, for which Britain built the impressive White City Stadium and planned an ambitious array of events, many having a particularly British flavour – indeed several were entered by no other nation – as did the judges, other officials and the rules.

Trouble began at the opening ceremony. The Finnish team had been allocated the Russian flag, so chose to march with no flag at all. The Swedish boycotted the ceremony because their flag had not been included in those flying above the stadium. The Americans responded to a similar oversight by refusing to dip their flag to the Royal Box. Worse was to come. Discrepancies in the rules of competition in Britain and the USA led to a re-run of the Men's 400m in which a single (British) athlete competed – and won gold – due to a boycott by the other (American) finalists. Meanwhile the French football team, reeling with shock at their 17-1 semi-final defeat at Denmark's hands, withdrew and refused to compete for bronze.

The Marathon event passed into legend. Its length was determined by the distance from Windsor Castle to the stadium's Royal Box, and well-wishers lined the route offering 'refreshment' to the competitors: at least one was forced to retire having drunk more champagne than is usual for an athlete during a race. The winner, Italian Pietri Dorando, proceeded in the wrong direction on entering the stadium, and was helped across the line by British officials to the fury of the Americans, whose Johnny Hayes was next to finish, unaided. Dorando was reluctantly disqualified but his being awarded a special cup can have done nothing to heal a fast-developing Anglo-American rift.

It might be hoped that, by the end of 1909, the British had developed a humbler perspective. A stubborn and often brutal refusal to consider the rights of women to vote, despite the growing strength of the Labour movement, suggests otherwise. The decade to come would provide a sterner lesson.

Irish philanthropist, and founder and director of homes for destitute children, Dr Thomas John Barnardo. **1900**

The new Hammersmith Workhouse, London, pictured in the early years of the 20th Century. The site still serves as Hammersmith Hospital, although many of the original buildings have now been replaced or much altered. Of the workhouse, only the administrative block survives.

1900

The Cabinet Room at
10 Downing Street
at the turn of the century.
1900

The noted trades unionist and London's first Labour Mayor Mr Will Crooks, seen here in his home borough of Poplar, London with his second wife, Elizabeth. Among his many social reform achievements was the Infant Life Protection Bill, which ended baby-farming in London.

1901

King Edward VII
in Scottish dress.
1901

Winston Churchill, in
a portrait taken when
he first took his seat in
the House of Commons.
1901

General view of the huge
crowd of over 114,000 who
assembled at the Crystal
Palace to watch the FA Cup
Final, Tottenham Hotspur v
Sheffield United.
20th April, 1901

The original Bank, City and South London tube station near Mansion House.
1st August, 1901

Actress Maude Adams, most noted for her signature role of Peter Pan.
1902

A section of Ibrox Park terracing collapsed during a friendly match between England and Scotland, causing the deaths of 25 people and injuries for over 500 more.
5th April, 1902

Muriel Robb, Wimbledon
Ladies' Singles champion.
5th June, 1902

The Surrey right wing takes
the ball away in a hockey
match with Sussex.
1903

Ada Reeve, whose acting career began in 1878, when she was four years old, in the pantomime 'Red Riding Hood' in Whitechapel and continued as a teenager in music hall. Her last performance was in the film 'A Passionate Stranger', 1957, when she was in her eighties.
1903

Emmeline Pankhurst, the
founder of the Women's
Social and Political Union,
and a leading light in the
suffragette struggle to gain
women the vote.
1st March, 1903

Sir Henry Evelyn Wood is promoted to the rank of Field Marshal. Sir Evelyn fought in the Crimean War, the Anglo-Zulu War and the Boer War, and was awarded the Victoria Cross in India in 1858.

8th April, 1903

Dorothea Douglass, Wimbledon Ladies' Singles champion in 1903, 1904, 1906, 1910, 1911, 1913 and 1914. Author of 'Tennis For Ladies', 1910, one of only two women (the other was Stefi Graf, French Open 1988) to win a Grand Slam singles final without losing a game; 6-0, 6-0, Wimbledon 1911.

5th June, 1903

Dan Gumbrell, a typical English farm worker, lighting his pipe whilst taking a break during the wheat harvest.
1st September, 1903

Facing page: Mr Richardson (in white hat) and the team of oxen he handled for 38 years during the wheat harvest at Lades Farm, Falmer, near Brighton, on the South Downs. The oxen, a rarity even in 1903, were later sold by the farmer's heir. Oxen were used in Sussex into the late 1920s.
1st September, 1903

The England team that
toured Australia and brought
back The Ashes.
1st November, 1903

Queen Alexandra with seven
of her grandchildren.
1904

Rolls-Royce co-founder,
Frederick Henry Royce.
1904

Julia Marlowe, the English-born American actress, famed for her Shakespearean roles.
1904

Carl Hagenbeck, considered the father of the modern zoo for his introduction of 'natural' animal enclosures modelled on animals' native habitats.
1904

Trams running along the
Victoria Embankment. The
ancient Egyptian stele, taken
from Egypt and known as
Cleopatra's Needle, can be
seen in the background.
1st February, 1904

Manchester City's winning
team for the FA Cup Final,
played against Bolton
Wanderers.
23rd April, 1904

General view of the action in the Sunderland goalmouth in a Football League Division One match with Aston Villa.
1st October, 1904

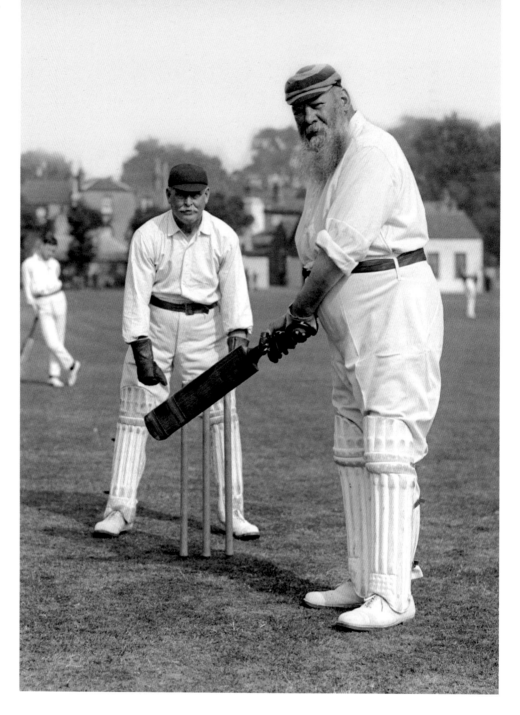

The cricketer W G Grace. He played in the first Test match in England – against Australia in 1880 at the Oval – and scored the first Test century by an English batsman. He died in 1915.
1905

King Edward VII and Queen
Mary on holiday in the
Austro-Hungarian Spa town
of Marienbad. The town now
lies in the Carlsbad region of
the Czech Republic.
1905

French artist and sculptor
Auguste Rodin, a regular
visitor to Britain.
1905

The Prince of Wales (later
George V) visiting the
Phoenix tin mine at Poldice
in Cornwall.
1905

Kaiser Wilhelm II, the last
German Emperor and King
of Prussia.
1905

Walter Crane, English
artist of the Arts and Crafts
movement.
1905

An artist at work, possibly
Angus Lindsay Calder.
1905

Henry Ainley, English
Shakespearean stage and
screen star, and father of
Anthony Ainley who played
'The Master' in BBC TV's
'Doctor Who'.
1905

Frank Brangwyn, Welsh artist and illustrator. Best known for the British Empire Panels, a work commissioned for the Houses of Parliament but refused because it was 'too exotic', now housed in the Brangwyn Hall, Swansea.
1905

William McGregor, Football
League President.
1st June, 1905

George Bernard Shaw attends a socialist rally as part of the Fabian Society, of which he was a founding member.
1st June, 1905

The competitors in the first
South Coast Motor Rally
Championship outside
Warne's Hotel, Worthing,
Sussex.
1st June, 1905

Celtic FC.
1st August, 1905

Goodison Park,
home of Everton FC.
1st August, 1905

Third Lanark team with the
Scottish Cup, which they
won by beating Rangers in
the replayed final.
1st August, 1905

Manchester United
Secretary Ernest Mangnall.
2nd September, 1905

Bill 'Fatty' Foulke, Chelsea goalkeeper. When playing for Sheffield in the 1902 Cup Final Foulke famously, angrily, nakedly and allegedly pursued the referee, a Mr Kirkham, who took refuge in a broom cupboard, in protest at his allowing the opposing team's equalising goal.
11th September, 1905

Stamford Bridge, home of
Chelsea, during a match
against West Bromwich
Albion.
23rd September, 1905

Fratton Park, home of
Southern League Division
One club, Portsmouth FC.
30th September, 1905

Preston North End take a
throw in playing against
Nottingham Forest.
30th September, 1905

New Zealand's Ernest
'General' Booth (R) races
forward with the ball. Rugby
Union, Somerset v New
Zealand at Jarvis's Field,
Taunton.
21st October, 1905

New Zealand squad
for their 1905-06 tour
of Great Britain.
1st November, 1905

The Masters take on the Old
Etonians in the Field Game,
Eton College.
30th November, 1905

Wales' team group for their
match against New Zealand
during their tour of Great
Britain.
16th December, 1905

Stage star Edna May outside
the Bedford Hotel, Brighton,
while she was 'resting' after
her retirement from 'The
Belle of Mayfair' because
of Camille Clifford's name
being printed larger than her
own on placards.
1906

A member of the 'Butterflies', a boy and girl acrobat troupe, sits by the window to take advantage of the bright sunshine for her sewing.
1906

London Hospital in
the East End of London.
1906

Facing page: Fribourg &
Treyer, the oldest snuff
shop in London.
1906

Italian opera singer Ada
Giachetti, outside the Savoy
Hotel with her teacher.
1906

Luisa Tetrazzini, an Italian
coloratura soprano, making
a record at the Gramophone
Office.
1906

Sir Hedworth Lambton, an English naval officer famous for bringing help to the British forces in the Siege of Ladysmith. He became Admiral of the Fleet during the First World War.
1906

Actress Edna May opens
a bazaar at Ealing.
1906

American millionaire Oscar
Lewisohn, the husband
of actress Edna May.
1906

George Clausen, English artist. A founder member of the New English Art Club, Clausen became Professor of Painting at the Royal Academy in 1906 and was knighted in 1927.

1906

Conservative politician Sir
Frederick Banbury (C),
campaigning successfully
for the City of London
parliamentary seat, at
Smithfield.
1st February, 1906

Everton's winning side in
the FA Cup Final against
Newcastle United.
21st April, 1906

Victor Trumper, the famous
and flamboyant Australian
batsman.
1st June, 1906

The semi-finalists in the
British Ladies' Amateur Golf
Championships at Burnham:
(L-R) Mrs Kennion (eventual
winner), Miss Cambell,
Mrs Simster and Miss
Thompson.
1st June, 1906

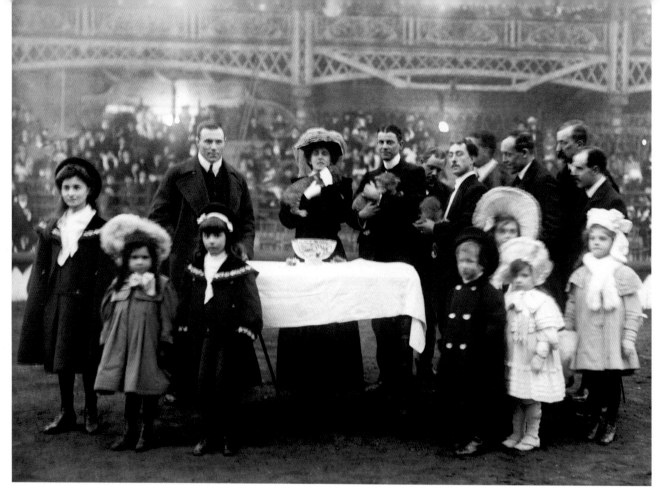

Professional wrestler
and strongman Georg
Hackenschmidt at
Olympia with baby lions.
Hackenschmidt was
nicknamed 'The Russian
Lion'.
1st June, 1906

Renowned English cricketer, Mr Pelham Francis Warner (better known as Plum Warner, the Grand Old Man of English Cricket), is watched closely by his Jack Russell.

1st June, 1906

The England cricket team bound for New Zealand, pictured by the 'Corinthie'. The MCC first sent a team to New Zealand in this year.
20th October, 1906

Facing page: Ladies during a tennis party at celebrity Edna May's wedding. Edna May retired from the stage after marrying her American millionaire: following her final appearance some of her (many) male admirers unhitched the horses from her carriage and pulled it to the Ritz, where she was dining that night, themselves.
1st August, 1906

May Sutton, later May Sutton Bundy, the first American to win the Wimbledon Women's Singles championship (in 1905) pictured in 1907, in which year she won it for the second time. Her scanty apparel shocked British audiences by revealing her wrists and ankles.
1907

Facing page: Sainsbury's Guildford High Street store on its opening day, typical of the counter service shops opened by Sainsbury's from the 1890s until 1939. The tiled walls, marble-topped counter and ceramic floor formed an instantly-recognisable 'house style' which was functional as well as decorative.
16th November, 1906

J R MacDonald MP (Ramsay MacDonald), later to become Britain's first Labour Prime Minister.
1907

King Edward VII and
Queen Alexandra
at Cowes, Isle of Wight.
1907

British philosopher and
pacifist, Bertrand Russell,
Third Earl Russell.
1907

French fashion designer
Coco Chanel in London.
1907

The 'Nimrod' at East India
docks. This was the ship
chosen by the British
Imperial Antarctic Expedition
under Ernest Shackleton.
1907

Suffragettes in an
underground garage leading
to the House of Commons.
1907

Trades unionist, activist and
one of the first Labour MPs,
Mr William Thorne (centre
L) and William Charles
Steadman, the Liberal MP
and Parliamentary Secretary
of the TUC.
1907

Facing page: Mr George
Nicoll Barnes (with Gladstone
bag), Scottish politician and
Labour Party MP.
1907

Attending a meeting of the
Labour Party Committee are,
from left, James O'Grady,
William Crooks and Mr B
Cooper of the L.C.C.
1907

Mr William 'Will' Thorne,
prominent trades unionist
and Labour MP.
1907

Territorial Army officers and
guards from the Military
School of Instruction at
Chelsea, on manoeuvres on
Wimbledon common.
1907

Vice President Charles
Warren Fairbanks of the
United States of America.
1907

Agnes Warner, wife of
English cricketer, Pelham
'Plum' Warner, with one
of their children.
1907

Kitty Marion, a German born English actress and an active member of the Women's Social and Political Union (WSPU). Imprisoned several times for militant activity.

1907

Packing a Short Brothers
balloon onto a horse-drawn
trailer, for a test flight by the
British Army.
1907

British Army soldiers
preparing a Short Brothers
balloon for flight.
1907

The London-born composer
Isidore de Lara, with the first
draft of his opera 'Solea'.
1907

John D Rockefeller, an
American industrialist and
philanthropist. Rockefeller
revolutionized the petroleum
industry, becoming the
world's richest man and first
U.S. dollar billionaire.
1907

Jacob Epstein, the American-born sculptor who worked chiefly in the UK, where he pioneered modern sculpture.
1907

Knights in chainmail armour
playing with a diabolo during
the Lord Mayor's Show.
1907

Dr Douglas Mawson, an Australian explorer, with fellow Antarctic explorer, Dr Ernest Shackleton. Mawson joined Shackleton's 'Nimrod' expedition, later turning down a place on Scott's 'Terra Nova' expedition to lead his own, of which he was to be the only survivor.
1907

Dr Alistair Forbes McKay,
Polar explorer and navy
surgeon, part of Ernest
Shackleton's 'Nimrod'
expedition to the South
Magnetic Pole.
1907

The ball is hacked clear from a corner during a match at Bank Street, home of Manchester United, which was won 2-1 by Portsmouth. 'All the time the struggle was waging the 30 Clayton chimneys smoked and gave forth their pungent odours, and the boilers behind goal poured mists of steam over the ground,' wrote *The Guardian* at the time.

16th January, 1907

A Labour Party
demonstration including
member Ramsey MacDonald
(C, bare-headed).
20th January, 1907

THE OXFORD CREW, 1907

The Oxford University crew
on the river during the Oxford
& Cambridge Boat Race.
1st March, 1907

Cardiff-born 'Peerless
Jim' Driscoll, British
Featherweight Champion.
1st April, 1907

Sheffield Wednesday's FA
Cup winning team, after
beating Everton for the
Championship.
20th April, 1907

The South African cricket
team that toured England.
15th May, 1907

American inventor
and businessman
Thomas Alva Edison.
1st June, 1907

May Sutton, Wimbledon
Ladies' Singles champion
in 1905 and 1907.
1st June, 1907

(L-R) Anthony Wilding
and Norman Brookes,
Wimbledon Men's Doubles
champions in 1907 (Wilding
won the Singles in 1910, and
Brookes won it in both 1907
and 1914).
10th June, 1907

The crowd watch the Henley
Regatta in progress.
6th July, 1907

General William Booth,
British Methodist preacher
who founded The Salvation
Army, speaking at Denby
Dale.
15th July, 1907

Army Dirigible No. 2, known as the 'Nulli Secundus II', about to take off. Designed by Col. John Capper of the Royal Engineers and Samuel Cody, she was built at the balloon factory at Farnborough. Parts of the crashed 'Nulli Secundus I' were used in this airship's construction.

1st July, 1908

The 'Nulli Secundus II' takes
to the air briefly.
24th July, 1907

The 'Nulli Secundus II', a semi-rigid military airship, left the ground five times but on each occasion a major problem forced the flight to be aborted. A contemporary report states: 'she pitched and tossed like some demented creature'. On the fifth landing further damage was incurred and no further attempts were made.
24th July, 1907

Vivian Woodward,
Tottenham Hotspurs and
England.
9th October, 1907

Facing page: The Lord
Mayor's coach as it passes
along Fleet Street at Temple
Bar, during the Lord Mayor's
Show.
1st November, 1907

The Lord Mayor's Show
Parade as it passes along
Fleet Street.
28th November, 1907

Members of the London Scottish Regiment celebrate Hogmanay at their barracks in Chelsea with tradional games such as 'Dookin for Apples'.
31st December, 1907

King Edward VII takes a stroll through the Austro-Hungarian Spa resort of Marienbad.
1908

Mrs Emmeline Pankhurst
(second R) with her daughter
Christabel and other
suffragette leaders at a
meeting at Clements Inn.
1908

Chief Inspector Scott (R),
Superintendant Taylor (C),
and Detective Inspector
Fowle, who have been
investigating the murder of
Caroline Luard, the wife of
Major-General Charles Luard.
1908

Major-General Charles Luard at the funeral of his wife, Caroline, who died of three gunshot wounds in their home – the 'Seal Chart Murder'. Major-General Luard was to commit suicide just a few weeks after his wife's murder, blaming rumours that he had killed her.
1908

Summer House, where
Caroline Luard's body was
found with three gunshot
wounds.
1908

The coroner at the 'Seal Chart Murder' inquest. Although Major-General Charles Luard was to commit suicide just a few weeks after his wife Caroline's murder, the inquest found she was killed 'by person or persons unknown'. The crime remains unsolved.
1908

Henry Hamilton Fyfe,
editor of the *Daily Mail*.
1908

Richard Bell (front row, C) was one of the first two British Labour Members of Parliament elected after the formation of the Labour Representation Committee in 1900. Bell was a high-profile trade unionist, the General Secretary of the Railway Servants union.
1908

Cricketing legend C B Fry
on crutches after injuring
one of his ankles badly while
playing for Sussex against
Middlesex.
1908

Flora Drummond (L) giving instructions to Suffragettes dressed as prisoners. Flora qualified as a postmistress but was not allowed to work in the trade as she was below the regulation height of 5 feet 2 inches. She was imprisoned nine times as a Suffragette and taught other inmates Morse code to communicate in the cells.
1908

Crowds watching a
Suffragette parade:
(L-R) Mrs Pankhurst,
Miss Clark, her sister,
the driver, Charlotte
Marsh and Jessie Kelly.
1908

Facing page: Suffragettes
conduct a procession after
their release from prison.
1908

Suffragette and WSPU
procession organiser,
the indomitable Flora
Drummond, known as
'The General'.
1908

Suffragettes outside Bow
Street.
1908

Suffragette activist Vera
Wentworth, who, after a spell
in prison where she went on
hunger strike, later accosted
Asquith, jostling him outside
a church then cornering him
with Herbert Gladstone on
a golf course.
1908

Actress Eva Moore (L) in
a Suffragette procession.
1908

Suffragette Emmeline
Pethick Lawrence
on her release from
Holloway Prison.
1908

Writer and artist Laurence
Houseman speaking in
Trafalgar Square during a
Suffragette demonstration.
He was the brother of the
poet A E Houseman.
1908

Christabel Pankhurst sitting
to John Tussaud (Madame
Tussaud's great-grandson)
for her model in wax.
1908

Barbara Ayrton (L), whose mother was the distinguished physicist, mathematician and Suffragette Hertha Ayrton. As Barbara Gould, Miss Ayrton would later become MP for Hendon North in Labour's landslide victory of 1945.
1908

Sculptor Edouard Lanteri, born in France, but later took up British nationality. He was the Professor of Modelling at South Kensington Art School.
1908

Facing page: Winston Churchill pays off a taxi.
1908

The yacht 'Mariska' (L),
passing 'HMS Agamemnon'
at Cowes.
1908

Tzar Nicholas II's black-hulled 5557 ton yacht 'The Standart' (R), at Cowes. Measuring 401 feet in length, the 'Standart' was the largest privately-owned vessel in the world.

1908

George Chirgwin, British
music hall entertainer,
applying blackface make up.
1908

Suffragette Dr Marion Phillips, Labour Party politician and elected Member of Parliament for Sunderland in 1929.
1908

A view of St Batholomews
Hospital in London.
15th January, 1908

A Suffragette procession
passing through Parliament
Square, London.
19th March, 1908

Sir Henry Campbell-Bannerman, who resigned as Prime Minister due to ill-health to be succeeded by Herbert Henry Asquith.
5th April, 1908

Wolverhampton Wanderers'
FA Cup winning team: (back
row, L-R) Rev Kenneth
Hunt, Jackery Jones,
Billy Wooldridge, Tommy
Lunn, Ted Collins, Albert
Bishop: (front row, L-R) Billy
Harrison, Jack Shelton,
George Hedley, Walter
Radford, Jack Pedley.
25th April, 1908

HMS Gladiator in shallow water off the Isle of Wight. During a late snowstorm, Gladiator was heading into Portsmouth Harbour when it struck the outbound American steamer SS Saint Paul. The American boat remained afloat and launched lifeboats, but the Gladiator foundered at once. 128 crew were lost and only three bodies were recovered.

26th April, 1908

King Edward VII and Queen Alexandra at the Duke of York's School.

24th May, 1908

Arthur Balfour opens the
Knebworth golf links.
1st June, 1908

Facing page: A view of
the Royal Box at the
International Horse Show
held at Olympia.
1st June, 1908

The International Archery
meeting, held at Ranelagh,
one of the most ancient of
women's sports.
1st June, 1908

Facing page: People enjoy
the sun on Yarmouth sands.
1st June, 1908

English cricketer W G Grace.
1st June, 1908

Anthony Asquith, son of H
H Asquith, Prime Minister,
looks over a barrier as a
policeman recovers his toy
aeroplane.
1st June, 1908

Mahatma Ghandi and friend
in South Africa as part of a
delegation of British Indians.
1st June, 1908

'Synorinetta', with jockey
Billy Bullock, being led in
after winning the Epsom
Derby.
1st June, 1908

Charlotte Sterry, Wimbledon Ladies' Singles Champion in 1895, 1896, 1898, 1901 and 1908.
10th June, 1908

Facing page: A posed picture in front of two balloons at a party in Winchester.
12th June, 1908

London Olympics: General
view of the White City
stadium during the Olympics.
24th July, 1908

London Olympics: The Great Britain team parades around the White City stadium during the opening ceremony.

27th April, 1908

London Olympics: The gold medal-winning Roehampton (Great Britain) polo team: (L-R) Charles Miller, Patteson Nickalls, George Miller, Herbert Wilson. The tournament was contested at the Hurlingham Polo Grounds and was entered by just two English and one Irish teams, ensuring a British victory.
21st June, 1908

Facing page: A crowd of people attend a demonstration in Hyde Park in favour of women's suffrage.
28th June, 1908

London Olympics: Dorothea
Lambert-Chambers takes on
Dora Boothby in the Ladies'
Singles Tennis Final.
7th July, 1908

Under-Secretary of State
for the Colonies Winston
Churchill arrives at Number
10 Downing Street with John
Morley, Secretary of State
for India.
7th July, 1908

London Olympics: The Great Britain clay pigeon team who won gold: (back row, L-R) John Postans, James Pike, Peter Easte: (front row, L-R) Alexander Maunder, Frank Moore, Charles Palmer.
9th July, 1908

London Olympics: Gold
medallists Reggie Doherty
and George Hillyard take on
Josiah Ritchie and James
Cecil Parke in the Men's
Outdoor Doubles final at the
All England Club.
10th July, 1908

London Olympics: General
view of the individual Rapid-
fire Pistol competition at
Bisley.
11th July, 1908

London Olympics: The USA
team, gold medallists in the
Team Military Rifle event.
11th July, 1908

London Olympics: Action
from the 20km Track Cycling
final.
14th July, 1908

London Olympics: The start of the 1500m final. Olympic records were set twice during this event, gold going to the USA's Mel Sheppard, silver to Great Britain's Harold A Wilson and bronze to Norman Hallows, also of Great Britain.

14th July, 1908

London Olympics: Great Britain's George Larner strides home to win gold in the 3500m Walk.
14th July, 1908

London Olympics: Matthew McGrath, USA, silver medallist in the Hammer event.
14th July, 1908

London Olympics: Robert Zimmerman, Canada, in the Springboard Diving event.
14th July, 1908

London Olympics: The
Great Britain team break
the tape to win the first
Three-Mile Team Race heat:
(L-R) Harold Wilson, Arthur
Robertson, Joe Deakin, Bill
Coales.
14th July, 1908

London Olympics: France's
Maurice Schilles and Andre
Auffray, gold medallists in
the 2000m Tandem event.
15th July, 1908

London Olympics:
The Polytechnic Ladies
put on a display in
the Gymnastics.
15th July, 1908

London Olympics: The
France team perform their
routine in the Gymnastics.
15th July, 1908

London Olympics: A team of
ladies representing Denmark
put on a display in the
Gymnastics.
15th July, 1908

London Olympics: Martin Sheridan, USA, gold medallist in the Men's Discus event.
16th July, 1908

Facing page: London Olympics: Victor Johnson, Great Britain, gold medallist in the 600m Track Cycling event.
15th July, 1908

London Olympics: Great Britain's George Larner (R) shakes hands with compatriot Ernest Webb (L), gold and silver medallists respectively in both the 3500m Walk and the 10 Mile Walk.

17th July, 1908

London Olympics: Lady
archers in competition.
Great Britain swept the
board in women's archery in
this year, largely due to no
other nation sending female
archers.
17th July, 1908

London Olympics: General
view of the competition.
Archery – Men's York
Round.
17th July, 1908

London Olympics: Jacques Rodocanachi, France, unplaced in the Individual Épée event.
17th July, 1908

London Olympics: Gaston
Alibert, France, gold
medallist in the Individual
Épée event.
24th July, 1908

London Olympics: General view of the competitors before the start of the final of the Cycling 100km Track event.

18th July, 1908

London Olympics: Great Britain's Charles Bartlett (R) comes home to win gold in the Cycling 100km Track event.
18th July, 1908

London Olympics: Athletes leap through the water jump in the Men's 3200m Steeplechase event.
18th July, 1908

London Olympics: Great Britain's Arthur Russell breaks the tape to win gold from compatriot Arthur Robertson (L) in the Men's 3200m Steeplechase event.
18th July, 1908

London Olympics: The competitors dive in at the start of the 200m Breaststroke final.
18th July, 1908

London Olympics: Great
Britain's Frederick Holman
touches first to win
gold in the Men's 200m
Breaststroke.
18th July, 1908

London Olympics: Charles Bartlett, Great Britain, gold medallist in the Cycling 100km Track event.

18th July, 1908

London Olympics: The Great
Britain team, made up of the
City of London Police team,
who won the gold medal in
the Tug of War event.
19th July, 1908

London Olympics: Great
Britain's Timothy Ahearne in
action in the Standing Long
Jump heats.
20th July, 1908

London Olympics: (L-R) Great Britain's Theodore Just breaks the tape to win the 800m heat from Germany's Andreas Breynck. Just placed fifth in the Final, 3.6 seconds behind gold medallist Mel Sheppard (USA) who set a new Olympic and unofficial World record.
20th July, 1908

Facing page: London Olympics: USA's Ray Ewry clears the Men's Standing High Jump bar to win gold, his tenth Olympic gold in all (including two at the 1906 unofficial games). Ewry became a superb athlete despite contracting polio as a child, confounding predictions that he might be wheelchair-bound for life.
20th July, 1908

London Olympics: Great Britain's Stanley Bacon, who won gold, takes on compatriot George De Relwyskow in the final of the Middleweight Division Freestyle Wrestling event.
21st July, 1908

London Olympics: Finland's Verner Weckman (facing camera), who won gold, takes on compatriot Yrjo Saarela in the final of the Greco-Roman Wrestling, Light Heavyweight Division event.

22nd July, 1908

London Olympics: Action
from the Water Polo final,
Great Britain v Belgium, with
Great Britain wearing dark
caps.
22nd July, 1908

London Olympics: The Great
Britain team that won gold in
the Water Polo, featuring Paul
Radmilovic (back row, second
R). Radmilovic won gold
medals in 1906, 1908, 1912
and 1920, establishing a record
that was unbeaten until Steve
Redgrave won his fifth gold in
the 2000 Sydney Olympics.
22nd July, 1908

London Olympics: USA's
Francis Irons leaps to win
gold in the Long Jump, and
set a new Olympic record.
22nd July, 1908

London Olympics: USA's
Harry Porter clears the bar
to win gold in the High Jump.
22nd July, 1908

London Olympics: South
Africa's Reggie Walker is
carried shoulder high by his
jubilant countrymen after
winning gold in the 100m
final.
22nd July, 1908

London Olympics: Canada's
Robert Kerr is carried across
the stadium after winning
gold in the 200m final.
23rd July, 1908

London Olympics: Canada's
Robert Kerr (second L) runs
over the line to win the gold
medal in the 200m final. The
silver medal went to USA's
Robert Cloughen (L) and the
bronze to USA's Nathaniel
Cartnell (second R). Great
Britain's George Hawkings
(R) finished in fourth place.
23rd July, 1908

London Olympics: Sweden's Arvid Sandberg, bronze medallist in the High Board Diving event.
24th July, 1908

London Olympics: General
view of the crowd in the
White City stadium.
24th July, 1908

London Olympics: The USA's Edward Cooke, joint gold medallist, clears the bar in the final of the Pole Vault.

24th July, 1908

London Olympics: USA's
Alfred Gilbert clears the bar
at 3.71m to tie for the gold
medal.
24th July, 1908

London Olympics: Canadian
Ed Archibald competing
in the Pole Vault. He was
to take joint bronze medal
place.
24th July, 1908

London Olympics: HRH The Princess of Wales (white dress, by chair) at the start of the Marathon event at Windsor Castle.
24th July, 1908

London Olympics: The runners pass through the gates of Windsor Castle near the start of the Marathon event.

24th July, 1908

London Olympics: South Africa's Charles Hefferon (R), the eventual silver medallist, coming through Ruislip in the Marathon event.
24th July, 1908

Facing page: London Olympics: Cyclists monitor the Canadian runners as they pass through Windsor during the Marathon event.
24th July, 1908

London Olympics: USA's John Hayes, the eventual gold medallist, makes his way through Willesden.
24th July, 1908

London Olympics: USA's
John Hayes approaches the
finish line to win the Olympic
Marathon.
24th July, 1908

London Olympics: USA's
John Hayes, gold medallist
in the Marathon, shows
off his trophy as he is
carried around the White
City stadium on a table by
teammates.
24th July, 1908

London Olympics: Great Britain's Henry Taylor is carried shoulder-high around the White City stadium after swimming the final leg in the Men's 4x200m Freestyle to win gold.
24th July, 1908

London Olympics: The
Duchess of Westminster
hands out the Diplomas of
Special Merit.
25th July, 1908

London Olympics: Great Britain's Wyndham Halswelle crosses the line to win gold in the 400m. Halswelle was the only competitor in the re-run final after his two American rivals boycotted the race in protest at the disqualification of one of their compatriots in the first running of the final.

25th July, 1908

London Olympics: Queen Alexandra presents Great Britain's Wyndham Halswelle (L) his gold medal for winning the 400m.
25th July, 1908

London Olympics: Great
Britain's Wyndham Halswelle
walks off after being
presented with his gold
medal by Queen Alexandra.
25th July, 1908

London Olympics: USA's
Forrest Smithson, gold
medallist in the 110m
hurdles, poses for a picture
carrying a bible in protest at
having to race on a Sunday.
20th July, 1908

London Olympics: Eric Lemming of Sweden taking part in the Javelin event. Lemming eventually took the gold medal.
28th July, 1908

London Olympics: Alexander McCulloch, Great Britain, silver medallist in the Single Sculls at Henley.
28th July, 1908

London Olympics: Great
Britain (nearest to camera)
take on Hungary in Heat
One of the Coxed Eights
event at Henley.
29th July, 1908

London Olympics: General
view of the scenes at Henley
during the Coxed Eights final.
31st July, 1908

London Olympics: General view of the action as Great Britain, represented by the Leander club, beat Belgium to win gold in the Coxed Eights at Henley.
31st July, 1908

London Olympics: Lord
Desborough (second R)
makes a speech at the prize-
giving ceremony at Henley.
31st July, 1908

Facing page: A beach
scene at Margate.
1st August, 1908

Chancellor of the Exchequer,
David Lloyd George.
1st August, 1908

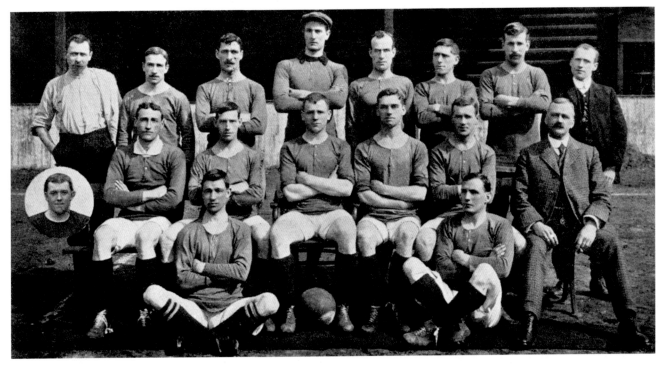

Manchester United squad 1908-09: (back row, L-R) Trainer F Bacon, Harold Halse, Billy Meredith, Harry Moger, John Picken, George Wall, George Stacey, Herbert Burgess (middle row, L-R) Sandy Turnbull, Jimmy Turnbull, Richard Duckworth, Charlie Roberts, Alex Bell, Vince Hayes, Secretary Ernest Mangnall: (front row, L-R) George Livingstone, Alex Downie.

1st August, 1908

'The Meteor' (L) and 'Zinita'
(R) compete in the race
across the Solent from the
Isle of Wight to the mainland
during Cowes week.
3rd August, 1908

London Olympics: 'Hera' and 'Mouchette', gold and silver medallists respectively and both representing Great Britain in the 12m Class, on the Clyde.
11th August, 1908

London Olympics: Great
Britain's Wolseley-Siddeley,
skippered by the Duke
of Westminster, in heavy
weather during the Open
Class Motor Boat event.
28th August, 1908

Will Thorne MP, leaving
a Trade Union meeting.
1st September, 1908

Mary Phillips, one of the
released Suffragettes, being
drawn along in a carriage.
1st September, 1908

Mary MacArthur, Secretary of the Women's Trade Union League, attends the Trades Union Congress meeting in Nottingham.
6th September, 1908

Labour Party founder James
Keir Hardie with his wife
Lillie.
9th October, 1908

Suffragette Emily Pankhurst
addressing a meeting in
Trafalgar Square.
11th October, 1908

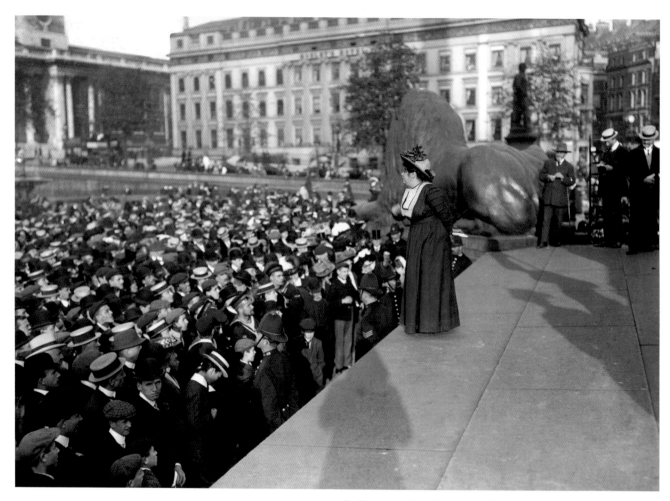

Suffragette Flora Drummond
addressing a gathering at
Trafalgar Square.
11th October, 1908

Keir Hardie's secretary, the Suffragette Margaret Travers Symons, who managed to enter the floor of the House while debate was in progress. Mrs Symons said a few words before being taken out, and became the first woman to speak there.
13th October, 1908

McClean and Brewer in the
'Britannia'. Gordon Bennett
Balloon Race.
8th October, 1908

British entrants Holland
Forbes and Post in 'The
Conqueror', before the
start of the Gordon Bennett
Balloon Race in Berlin,
Germany.
14th October, 1908

American aviator and pioneer of manned flight, Samuel Cody, seated in British Army Aeroplane No. 1 before testing at Farnborough.
16th October, 1908

British Army Aeroplane No. 1
is taken from its hanger
before making the first
British powered flight over
Farnborough Common.
16th October, 1908

British Army Aeroplane No. 1
is towed to its take-off point
on Farnborough Common.
16th October, 1908

London Olympics: Sweden's
Ulrich Salchow, gold
medallist and inventor of
the Salchow jump.
21st October, 1908

London Olympics: The Great Britain football team which won gold in the London Olympics football tournament at White City, beating Denmark 2-0 in the final. Earlier Denmark had beaten France by an astonishing 17-1. France were so shocked by this that they withdrew, refusing to compete for bronze.
24th October, 1908

London Olympics:
William Philo, Great Britain,
Middleweight gold medallist.
27th October, 1908

London Olympics: Action
from the Great Britain v
France hockey game.
29th October, 1908

London Olympics:
Germany's goalkeeper
Carl Ebert (R) is unable to
prevent Scotland scoring
one of their four goals in the
first round of the Hockey
event.
29th October, 1908

Jules Gautier, the manacled swimmer.
1909

Facing page: The Oxford and Cambridge Boat Race.
1909

Ramsey McDonald.
1909

Facing page: King
Edward VII, in German
uniform, and the German
Emperor, Kaiser Wilhelm II.
1909

10 Downing Street.
1909

President of the Board of
Trade Winston Churchill
(L) with Chancellor of the
Exchequer David Lloyd
George (R).
1909

Ladies at work
at Spring Hall Farm.
1909

Facing page: A remarkable
flying machine being
constructed at Taplow
by Scottish inventor, G L
Davidson. It is built in the
form of a bird and when
finished it will weigh over six
tons. It is designed to carry
twenty or thirty passengers
at speeds of up to 150mph.
1909

Famed American aviation pioneers Wilbur & Orville Wright show how to construct a wing of an aircraft, while at the Short Brothers' aeroplane factory at Shellbeach in Kent.
1909

A Suffragette procession.
1909

Suffragette Emmeline
Pethick-Lawrence's release
from Holloway Prison.
1909

Sidney Webb, a British
socialist, economist and
reformer, and early member
of the Fabian Society.
1909

Artist Tom Mostyn: born in
Liverpool in 1864, Mostyn
studied at the Manchester
Academy of Fine Arts and
was showing at the Royal
Academy by the age of 29.
1909

George Lansbury: politician,
socialist, Christian pacifist
and newspaper editor. He
was leader of the Labour
Party from 1932 to 1935.
1909

Andrew Bonar Law,
Conservative politician and
future Prime Minister.
1909

Clementine Churchill, the
wife of Winston Churchill, and
Lord Cheyllsmore, Mayor of
Westminster, at a bazaar in aid
of the Browning Settlement, at
the Horticulture Hall.
1909

Solomon Cutner, a child
prodigy of the piano,
commonly known as
'Solomon'.
1909

King Edward VII at Hall
Barn, Beaconsfield home of
Daily Telegraph proprieter
Lord Burnham.
1909

King Edward VII (L) with a
shooting party at Hall Barn.
1909

The beaters at the hunt, during the visit of King Edward VII and the Prince of Wales at Hall Barn, Beaconsfield, country home of Lord Burnham.
1909

Vivian Woodward, England.
Home International
Championship – England v
Wales.
15th March, 1909

James Braid drives a guttie
from the tee in a match at
Sandy Lodge to determine
the relative merits of the two
types of ball – the gutties
and the rubber cores. J H
Taylor (L) looks on.
1st April, 1909

The victorious Manchester
United team. F A Cup Final –
Manchester United v
Bristol City.
25th April, 1909

The Bristol City team that
lost the FA Cup Final to
Manchester United.
25th April, 1909

Jack Hobbs, Surrey
and England cricketer.
1st June, 1909

Suffragette Emmeline
Pankhurst (R) in prison
costume along with her
daughter Christabel.
1st June, 1909

The Princess of Wales
leaving a tin mine during
a royal visit to the west of
England.
1st June, 1909

A great crowd converges
upon Minoru, Herbert Jones
up, as he is led in by his
owner, King Edward VII,
after winning the Epsom
Derby.
2nd June, 1909

Dora Boothby, Wimbledon
Ladies' Singles champion.
9th June, 1909

Lieutenant-General and Inspector General of Cavalry, Robert Baden-Powell.
30th June, 1909

The Short Brothers
Aeronautical Engineers'
factory at Shellbeach, home
of the first aviation company
in the world.
1st July, 1909

Facing page: People
enjoying the sun on the cliffs
at Folkestone in Kent.
1st July, 1909

Judging the Wolfhound class
at the Richmond Dog Show.
23rd July, 1909

Tom Vardon with his caddie Ray during the Open Championship held at the Royal Cinque Ports Golf Club in Deal, Kent.
23rd July, 1909

Louis Bleriot makes the
first powered flight across
the English Channel,
winning a $5,000 prize
from Lord Northcliffe and
overshadowing longer flights
already made over land by
the Wright Brothers and
others. H G Wells wrote;
'England is no longer, from
a military point of view, an
inaccessible island'.
25th July, 1909

Boxers Jimmy Britt and
Johnny Summers signing a
contract.
1909

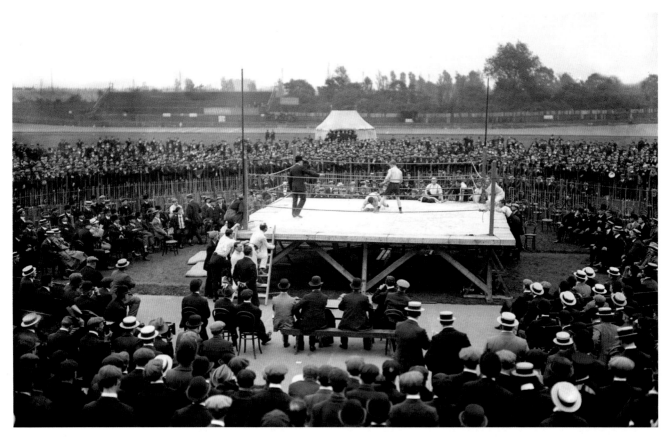

American boxer Jimmy
Britt fights Britain's Johnny
Summers in an open-air
contest in London.
31st July, 1909

Sam Langford, the
unofficial World 'Coloured'
Heavyweight Champion.
1st August, 1909

Peter McWilliam of
Newcastle United, who went
on to manage Tottenham
Hotspurs.
1st August, 1909

Queen Alexandra, King Edward VII, Prince George, Queen Mary, The Prince of Wales, Princess Mary, The Czar and Czarina of Russia, The Czaravitch of Russia and the Russian Grand Duchesses.
4th August, 1909

King Edward VII with his horse Minoru, the 1909 Derby Stakes winner.
1st September, 1909

Oxford University Rugby
Union team 1909-10.
1st October, 1909

Winston Churchill and
the German Emperor,
Kaiser Wilhelm II.
2nd October, 1909

Henri Farman, a French aviator of English descent, flying at a Blackpool meeting where he won the distance and duration prize of $10,000. In 1914 he founded the Farman Aviation Works that produced more than 12,000 military aircraft for France in the First World War.

20th October, 1909

Actress and author Nancy Price (R) and her young daughter Joan Maude, at the zoo. Price appeared in over 30 films and published 24 books of anecdotes, essays, novels, plays, autobiography and poems.
1st December, 1909